Taino Earthschooling in the Diaspora

My Early Days

Anani Kaike

Koki Medicine Clan

Copyright © 2014 Laura Adams
All rights reserved.
ISBN:0615992471
ISBN-13:978-0615992471

DEDICATION

This book is dedicated to my cousin Carlito who is in the Ancestral World. My cousin's life was cut short too young. I hold him strongly in my heart, and I trust we are always together. As long as I am in this world I will always hold my cousin in my heart. Here I am with Carlito and our beloved Taino Matriarch Grandmother "Mama Rosa".

CONTENTS

Acknowledgments

Foreword: Growing up Taino in the Diaspora

Earthschooling

Living With Ceremony

Conucos- Gardens

River Ceremony

Spiritual Baths

Plant Oils

Batey

Me

ACKNOWLEDGMENTS

I acknowledge my parents, who are teaching me so much, and who I love to my heart. I will always keep them in my heart. My parents have taught me how to love and honor my Ancestors, and have lead me to have a historical and global understanding of this world. I acknowledge Mother Earth for her life giving Rains and Soils. I acknowledge the Sun for its life giving rays, and the moon, stars and planets for their rhythms and dances.

Taino Earthschooling in the Diaspora: Perspective of the Elders

Growing up Taino in the Diaspora as children requires a consciousness from the parents as to the principles of Taino Indigenous Spirituality and Culture. The great Taino principles are both simple and profound, and are intrinsically intertwined with the practices of living in harmony with Mother Earth, the same basic principles as the many great nations of this Continent, Turtle Island. Living in the diaspora is inherently distinct from living on one of the Ancestral Taino islands of the Caribbean, and so a creative process must emerge of bringing forth Taino Spirituality and Culture within a vastly different place, climate, and seasonal pattern. As parents, grandparents and even great grandparents, we must use all of our hard lessons and struggles, to give our future generations the best of the fruits and roots of our lifetimes.

We utilize the term "Earthschooling" to describe our practices of "homeschooling" our children. Earthschooling is about cultivating the child's understanding, appreciation and deep relationship with Mother Earth, Atabey. Earthschooling includes language, history, culture, horticulture, science, astronomy, geography, art and all the usual subjects one would experience in school. However, Earthschooling teaches these in the context of our Taino Culture and Tradition, and most significantly within the context of the great Taino Principles of Living and Thriving upon Mother Earth. Our children become Earth-rooted through their process of Earth-Schooling, fundamentally understanding their place within the Earth and within the River of Time.

Our daughter, Anani Kaike at the age of 8 years old, has a profound mind and spirit. Unlike many of the older generation, she was born within the reclaiming of our Taino Identity (Taino Resurgence), and she was born with Ceremonies from when she was in the womb, to her birth, to her blessing Ceremony and the planting of her placenta. She took her first steps in the Bateys and Ceremonial Lands that her Elders caretake, and represents the generation of children who no longer need to think of reclaiming, but who take that "reclaiming" to the new dimension of "embodying". Her name is Taino and means "Flower of the Water who Nourishes the Earth".

This book is the first in a series of books that she will be bringing forth to share her experiences of Earthschooling. It is an overview of some of the many Cultural and Spiritual Components that make up her Earthschooling. It is also a fruit of her Earthschooling as she finds her voice to express her identity as a Taino Child growing up in the Diaspora!

EARTH SCHOOLING

Earthschooling is about being connected with the Earth. It is about loving Mother Earth and learning her ways. We learn her ways by OBSERVING and LISTENING with our Spirit and our Heart!

Spirit is Creation.   There is Spirit in the Forest and Mountains, there is Spirit in the Rivers, Oceans and Valleys. Spirit lives where ever you look. Spirit lives in everyone. Spirit lives in You!

Earthschooling is about loving the Ancestors. The Ancestors are the Elders who are in the "Other World", the World of the Dead. Ancestors are the Grandmothers and Grandfathers, Aunts, Uncles, Cousins, Sisters and Brothers who have come before us. They are our Family Tree whose Roots go deep into the Earth.

All Ancestors are connected to the same web, but Ancestors have different stories to tell. In my family our story is Taino and many Ancestors have come to be connected to our Taino web. I want to share some of my Taino stories.

Taino is the Indigenous People of the Caribbean Islands. Taino people garden, hunt, fish, build homes and special places for Ceremony called Bateys, all in ways that are gentle to Mother Earth. They lived in peace with Mother Earth and all her many children, the four leggeds, creepy crawlers, the fliers, the swimmers, the green ones and the two leggeds (us). All Taino children were Earthschooled by their Elders.

Earthschooling has taught me that my Taino People were gentle to the Earth but that did not mean that they were not fierce and brave warriors! When you hear people talk about Taino being the "gentle and good people" that is about our love and gentleness for Mother Earth and all her Children.

In my family we do many things that are about Healing the Spirit. We care about healing the relationship between People and Mother Earth, and between People and their Ancestors. We care about bringing the Ancestors back to peace. We also care about healing Mother Earth. We give Mother Earth fertility, we give her Offerings, we do Ceremonies for her, and we plant many Trees, Bushes and Plants. We clean her streams, pick up trash, and make special places where the Spirit can be happy.

LIVING WITH CEREMONY

At the heart of Living with Ceremony is the relationship between the Living and the Dead. The Living is Us and the Plants, the Animals, and all of life that grows and breathes. The Dead is the Ancestors and all that decays and becomes soil for Mother Earth.

Life is a Cycle that has Life and Death inside it. Think of a seed that germinates (sprouts) in the soil. It grows to be a seedling, then to a sapling, then to a tall tree. One day the tree gets old or a big windy thunderstorm comes and knocks the tree down. The tree decays and becomes soil. It becomes "The Dead" and it helps other seeds grow!

We care about the Dead because that is what allows our life to be abundant. We also care about the Dead because we love our Ancestors who came before us and who we will one day become.

Living with Ceremony is sometimes about giving the Ancestors an Arieto (big feast). Sometimes it is about planting seeds in the garden or it is about planting a special tree for an Ancestor with sacred ingredients under its roots. Sometimes it is remembering a dream and meditating on what the dream means. Almost always Ceremony is about healing someone or something.

CONUCOS – GARDENS

Conucos (Gardens) are very important to us. Conuco is a Taino word which is about the mounded gardens that my Taino Ancestors made. Gardens are the place where we express our Spirit with the Earth and the Earth expresses her Spirit with Us. We grow food, herbs, medicines, and flowers in our gardens. Gardens are very important in Earthschooling. We learn about plants and animals in the gardens.

We learn about the tiny living creatures that live in the soil and help the plants grow. Soil is full of Life. There are important microorganisms (tiny living things) in the soil and fungi that help the soil give life to the plants. They help decay the fallen tree, and they help the plants take in nutrition. When chemicals are thrown on the soil, this kills this important life and the soil is not fertile. Soil fertility is the most important foundation for a beautiful garden.

There are also many important insects, like bees, wasps and good flies that help the flowers pollenate and they also eat insects that harm the plants. This is why we plant many herbs and flowers that attract these helpful insects. We never plant just one kind of plant because then the helpful insects can't protect it. We give them what they need so they can help us.

In the garden I plant seeds, I water the garden, I make prayers, I sing, I rattle, and I harvest vegetables, fruits and herbs. One of my favorite things to do in the garden is to snack on all the berries and veggies that are growing. They taste better fresh from the plant than from the store.

Water is very important for the garden. All life needs water to grow. There is no life without water. This is why we do special ceremony with the Rain, River and Ocean.

River Ceremony

I have been going to the River since before I could walk and this great Spirit of the River is very significant to me because my name means "Flower of the Water". The River collects all the water that comes from the Rain that falls on the Earth and carries it to the Ocean. The Sun warms the Ocean and the water vapor rises up and eventually becomes Rain.

We go to the River to give the River offerings and to refreshen our Spirits in the Water. I sit by the river to meditate and to feel the Spirit of the River and the Spirit of the River feels me too!

The River is always moving and talking. Sometimes we see fish, which is a very good sign. We also find many interesting plants which grow along the river. These are good plants for making into Spiritual Baths. I was very excited last year to find mountain mint next to the River.

The River joins the Ocean at a place where we say the "Two Waters Meet." Here I am in the Bay where the River flows into the salty waters of the Ocean. My Taino Ancestors were very talented fishers who fished in the Rivers and Oceans and both waters are essential to us.

SPIRITUAL BATHS

I love to gather flowers and leaves to make fragrant baths. I have been doing this with my Elders for as long as I remember. They are so refreshing and energizing. My Spirit gets so excited when I gather the flowers and make the baths.

Some baths chase away negativity. Other baths bring sweetness and harmony. I can make a bath to bring strength or calmness as well. I have made many baths for adults who appreciate receiving this gift, and I am happy to share the wisdom my Spirit carries.

First I gather the flowers or leaves. I like to use very fragrant plants. There are many trees that also have very fragrant flowers and leaves. I use flowers from small plants, bushes and trees for my baths. These flowers all come from my own Garden that I have had since I was in my Mother's Womb.

Next I put all the plants into the water and I rub them vigorously to release the fragrance into the water. I add other natural ingredients. Then the bath sits in the Sun and under the Moonlight and Starlight. My Mother or Father blows Tobacco smoke into the Bath. I rattle and sing also. It is important that the bath sit in the lights of the Sun and Moon because this brings more strength to the bath. It is the best in the warm weather when I can do this outside.

My favorite part is when I pour the water over my head as I stand in the Garden among all the plants and then I sit in the Sun to dry off!

PLANT OILS

Oil is a way to pull out the powerful parts of the plants so they can be used to help us. The Spirit of the Plant goes into the Oil and then we can use that oil for Ceremony, for Healing, and for massage.

I use many of the plants I grow to create these oils. By now we have hundreds of plant oils in our home. One of my favorites is lavender, but there are many more that I make.

First I gather the plants which is always fun because there are always insects and interesting things to see. Then I use my pilon (mortar and pestle) to grind up the plants with a little oil. I like to use Olive Oil, Apricot Oil, Avocado Oil, Sesame Oil, Coconut Oil and any other healthy oil. I always say, "don't put something on your body that you are not willing to eat!"

Next I add the plants with the oil into a glass bottle. I never use plastic because it has chemicals that could go into the oil. The oil needs to sit for a few months while the oil pulls the Spirit from the plant. Then I can strain the oil and use it.

BATEY

Batey is a Ceremonial Space with stones and petroglyphs. Petroglyphs are stone drawings. Taino petroglyphs are ancient and show the Spirits of many things, like the Huricane (Hurakan), the Sun, the Moon, Ancestors, Plant Spirits and Animal Spirits. We have many Bateys on our Land. Some are in the forest and some are in the open. Some have gardens around them.

Batey is also where the Taino played an Ancient Taino ball game called Batu. The Batu was a sacred ceremonial game. There are many huge Bateys in the Caribbean, especially in my Ancestral home Boriken where the greatest Bateys have been uncovered.

Ever since I was a baby I love to play and dance in the Batey. My Elders light Sacred Fires in the Batey and then I can rattle and meditate. It takes concentration to meditate because there are lot of distractions. I like to look into the fire when I meditate because then the distractions go away.

 I get to play in the Bateys when we are not doing Ceremony as long as I am respectful. It is very important to be respectful of Spirit. It is my responsibility to teach other children who come here, like my nieces and nephews and cousins, to also be respectful. Sometimes I even have to remind Adults to be respectful. Other children love to come to the Bateys and see the Petroglyphs and play in the Sacred Spaces.

Me

My name Anani Kaike means "Flower of the Water and Nourisher of the Earth." I am 8 years old and I am a Taino living in the Taino Diaspora. I am also African and European and have many ghosts in my blood whose stories come from distant shores.

I wrote this book to share the Wisdom of my Elders and the beauty and blessings of my Life. I wrote this book to share how it is to be Taino today, especially Taino who are far from our Ancestral Islands.

Earthschooling is a word my parents have coined to describe the education that I am living. I learn the regular subjects of math, science (which I love the best), reading and writing, but I also learn about all these spiritual and cultural realities. I learn directly from Mother Earth and all her Children, the many Spirits that call Earth "home".

I have a message of care-taking for Mother Earth that I want to bring forth. Our Ancestors know the importance of clean air, clean water, fertile soil, and harmonious living upon the Earth. I hear and see many examples of the abusing of Mother Earth, which hurts all of us. I see how many chemicals are thrown into the waters, and how much trash has been created that is poisoning the Soils and Waters. I learn about all the animals that have gone extinct, and are going extinct. I hear about how Great Forests like the Amazon and the Boreal Forests are cut and never replanted. These are just some of the reasons that I know it is important to remember how our Ancestors lived, and how our Ancestors are still guiding us to live. We are finding new ways to return to old ways. We are finding trees to plant, gardens to grow and Bateys to build.

I want to take a moment to remember my Great Grandmother, Carmela who became an Ancestor long before I was born. My father remembers when he was a child seeing his Grandmother, Carmela, comb her long grey hair. As she combed her hair she said over and over again, "I am Taina, my Mother was Taina, my Grandmother was Taina." This is a sacred memory and is about being Taino when it was not easy to be Taino, when a lot of people tried to hide that they were Taino. There was a lot of racism and oppression that the Taino Ancestors in my family had to endure. This is one of the reasons I am writing this book. Today, Taino is not whispered, it is shouted!

I am grateful that my Ancestors never gave up Our Taino Identity!

www.ingramcontent.com/pod-product-compliance
Lightning Source LLC
Chambersburg PA
CBHW041813040426
42450CB00001B/21